The Lady Contemplation by Margaret Cavendish

Part I (of II)

Margaret Lucas Cavendish, Duchess of Newcastle-upon-Tyne was born in 1623 in Colchester, Essex into a family of comfortable means.

As the youngest of eight children she spent much time with her siblings. Margaret had no formal education but she did have access to scholarly libraries and tutors, although she later said the children paid little attention to the tutors, who were there 'rather for formality than benefit'.

From an early age Margaret was already assembling her thoughts for future works despite the then conditions of society that women did not partake in public authorship. For England it was also a time of Civil War. The Royalists were being pushed back and Parliamentary forces were in the ascendancy.

Despite these obvious dangers, when Queen Henrietta Maria was in Oxford, Margaret asked her mother for permission to become one of her Ladies-in-waiting. She was accepted and, in 1644, accompanied the Queen into exile in France. This took her away from her family for the first time.

Despite living at the Court of the young King Louis XIV, life for the young Margaret was not what she expected. She was far from her home and her confidence had been replaced by shyness and difficulties fitting in to the grandeur of her surroundings and the eminence of her company.

Margaret told her mother she wanted to leave the Court. Her mother was adamant that she should stay and not disgrace herself by leaving. She provided additional funds for her to make life easier. Margaret remained. It was now also that she met and married William Cavendish who, at the time, was the Marquis of Newcastle (and later Duke). He was also 30 years her senior and previously married with two children.

As Royalists, a return to life in England was not yet possible. They would remain in exile in Paris, Rotterdam and Antwerp until the restoration of the crown in 1660 although Margaret was able to return for attention to some estate matters.

Along with her husband's brother, Sir Charles Cavendish, she travelled to England after having been told that her husband's estate (taken from him due to his being a royalist) was to be sold and that she, as his wife, would receive some benefit of the sale. She received nothing. She left England to be with her husband again.

The couple were devoted to each other. Margaret wrote that he was the only man she was ever in love with, loving him not for title, wealth or power, but for merit, justice, gratitude, duty, and fidelity. She also relied upon him for support in her career. The marriage provided no children despite efforts made by her physician to overcome her inability to conceive.

Margaret's first book, 'Poems and Fancies', was published in 1653; it was a collection of poems, epistles and prose pieces which explores her philosophical, scientific and aesthetic ideas.

For a woman at this time writing and publishing were avenues they had great difficulty in pursuing. Added to this was Margaret's range of subjects. She wrote across a number of issues including gender, power, manners, scientific method, and philosophy.

She always claimed she had too much time on her hands and was therefore able to indulge her love of writing. As a playwright she produced many works although most are as closet dramas. (This is a play not intended to be performed onstage, but instead read by a solitary reader or perhaps out loud in a small group. For Margaret the rigours of exile, her gender and Cromwell's closing of the theatres mean this was her early vehicle of choice and, despite these handicaps, she became one of the most well-known playwrights in England)

Her utopian romance, 'The Blazing World', (1666) is one of the earliest examples of science fiction. Margaret also published extensively in natural philosophy and early modern science; at least a dozen books.

She was the first woman to attend a meeting at Royal Society of London in 1667 and she criticized and engaged with members and philosophers Thomas Hobbes, René Descartes, and Robert Boyle.

Margaret was always defended against any criticism by her husband and he also contributed to some of her works. She also gives him credit as her writing tutor.

Perhaps a little strangely she said her ambition despite her shyness, was to have everlasting fame. During her career, from the mid 1650's until her death, she was prolific. In recent decades her work has undergone a resurgence of interest propelled mainly by her ground-breaking attitude and accomplishments in those male straitened times.

Margaret Cavendish died on 15th December 1673 and was buried at Westminster Abbey.

Index of Contents

THE ACTOR'S NAMES
Lord Title
Lord Courtship
Sir Experience Traveller
Sir Fancy Poet
Sir Golden Riches
Sir Effeminate Lovely
Sir Vain Complement
Sir Humphrey Interruption
Master Adviser
Doctor Practise, and other Gentlemen
Tom Purveyer
Roger Farmer
Old Humanity
Servants, and others
The Lady Contemplation
The Lady Conversation
The Lady Visitant
The Lady Ward
The Lady Virtue
Lady Amorous
Mrs. Troublesome
Mrs. Governess, the Lady Virtues Attendant
Nurse Careful, Nurse to Lady Ward
Maudlin Huswife, Roger Farmers wife
Mall Mean-bred, the daughter
Nan Scape-all, Maid to the Lady Virtue

[Enter the **LADY CONTEMPLATION**, and the **LADY VISITANT**.

LADY VISITANT
What Lady Contemplation, musing by your self alone?

LADY CONTEMPLATION
Lady Visitant, I would you had been ten miles off, rather than to have broken my Contemplation.

LADY VISITANT
Why, are you so godly, to be so serious at your Devotion?

LADY CONTEMPLATION
No faith, they were Contemplations that pleas'd me better than Devotion could have done; for those that contemplate of Heaven, must have death in their mind.

LADY VISITANT
O no, for there is no Death in Heaven to disturb the joyes thereof.

LADY CONTEMPLATION
But we must dye before we come to receive those joyes; and the terrifying thoughts of Death, take away the pleasing thoughts of Heaven.

LADY VISITANT
Prethee let me know those pleasing thoughts.

LADY CONTEMPLATION
I did imagine my self such a Beauty, as Nature never made the like, both for Person, Favour, and Colour, and a Wit answerable to my Beauty, and my Breeding and Behaviour answerable to both, my Wisdome excelling all: And if I were not thus as I say, yet that every one should think I were so; for opinion creates more, and perfecter Beauties, than Nature doth. And then that a great powerful Monarch, such a one as Alexander, or Cæsar, fell desperately in love with me, seeing but my Picture, which was sent all about the world; yet my Picture (I did imagine) was to my disadvantage, not flattering me any wayes; yet this Prince to be inamoured with this shadow for the substance sake: Then Love perswaded him to send me his Picture, which represented him to the life, being extreamly handsome, yet had a manly and wise countenance. This Picture being brought by Embassadours, which Embassadours when they came, treated with me about marriage with this sole Emperor, all other Kings and Princes being but Tributaries; receiving these Embassadours with great civility and respect, yet behaving my self with a reserved and Majestical behaviour, which the Embassadours observing, said, I was the only Lady that was fit to be the only Emperours wife, both for my Beauty, Carriage, and Wit: When after a modest Fear, and seeming Humility, I had reason'd against the marriage, at last by their perswasion I consented; then was there Post after Post, and Messenger after Messenger, sent with letters from the Emperour to me, and from me to the Emperour; he admiring my letters, for the elegancy of the stile, and eloquency of

the wit, and admiring my Picture for the beauty; one while reading my letters, and another while viewing my Picture, made him impatient for my Company, which made him send to his Embassadours, that with all speed they should bring me away, sending to all the Princes whose Kingdomes I was to passe thorow, that they should guard me with Armyes, but not retard me with Olimpias, or the like, but to convey me safe and speedily: Whereupon I took my Journey (most of the Kingdome where I was born petitioning to wait on me); but by reason I could not take them all, unlesse I should depopulate the Kingdome, I would carry none, lest I should displease those that were to be left behind; but as I went out of the City where I dwelt, all the streets were strewed with dead Lovers, which had lived only on hopes, so long as I lived amongst them: But when they knew for certain I was to depart, their hopes vanished, and they dyed with despair. The Embassadours seeing such a Mortality, caused the Army that was my guard to march apace, and my Coaches to trundle away, thinking it was the Plague; but at last, after my Beauty had killed millions in the Kingdomes I passed thorow, I arrived at that part of the world where the Emperour was, who was a Joyed man to hear of my coming, and had made great preparations against my arrival; but some few dayes before my arrival, he sent a Chariot which was made of the thinnest plated gold, because it should be light in the Carriage, but the body of the Chariot was enameled and set with precious stones, the Horses trappings were only great Chains of pearls, but the horses reigns were Chains of gold, that might be strong enough to check their hot Spirits, and swift speed; as for my self, I was only cloathed in white Satin, and a Crown of Diamonds on my head, like a Bride, for I was to be marryed as soon as I met the Emperour; but as I past along, all the Highwayes were beset with Crouds of people, which thronged to see me, and when they saw me, they cryed out I was an Angel sent from the Gods; but your coming spoyl'd the Triumph, and brake the Marriage.

LADY VISITANT
No, no it is retarded for a time, the next musing Contemplation the marriage Nuptial will be.

LADY CONTEMPLATION
If you had not come and hinder'd me, I should have gover'nd all the world before I had left off Contemplating.

LADY VISITANT
But if you make such hast to be at the Government of the whole world, you would want a Theam for your thoughts to work upon, for you can aim at no more than all the world.

LADY CONTEMPLATION
O yes, rather than fail I would make new worlds, but this wil last me a long time in shewing you what wise Laws I make, what upright Justice I give, ordering so, as the whole world should be as one united Family; and when I had shewed my wisdome in Peace, then my thoughts should have raised Warres, wherein I would have shewed my valour and conduct.

LADY VISITANT
Prethee be not so imprudent to cast away precious time, and to bury thy life in fantasms.

LADY CONTEMPLATION
Why prethee, they manage time best, that please life most, For it were better not to be, than to be displeased; for there is none that truly lives, but those that live in pleasure, & the greatest pleasures is in the imagination not in fruition; for it is more pleasure for any person to imagin themselves Emperour of the whole world, than to be so; for in imagination they reign & Rule, without the troublesome and weighty cares belonging thereto; neither have they those fears of being betrayed or usurped as real

Emperours have; Besides, the whole general Race of Man-kind, may this way be the particular Emperour of the whole World, if they will; but those that desire to be Emperours any other wayes, have but sick judgements, for the mind is all, for if that be pleased, man is happy.

LADY VISITANT
Well, well, I had rather have the Material world, than you Airy Fictions.—But confess really to me, if you should not think your self accurst if you were to have no other Lovers, but what your Fancy creates.

LADY CONTEMPLATION
No truely, for I finding none so exact as my Fancy creates, makes all men appear worse than they are: For imagination doth like Painters, which takes all the gracefullest lines, and exactest Features from two or three good faces, and draws them into one: this is the reason that there may be handsomer Pictures drawn, than any Creature born; because, Nature distributes and divides her Favours, as to the generality, when Painter contract them into particulars; for there was never any, unlesse born as a wonder, that hath no exceptions; besides, my Lovers which my Fancy creates, never make me jealouse, nor never disturb me; come to me, and goe from me; speak or are silent as I will have them, and they are behaved, qualified, and adorned to my humour, also of what Birth, Age, Complexion, or Stature I like best; thus their persons and souls are created in my brain, live in my Contemplation, and are dead and buryed in my forgetfulnesse, but have a Resurrection in my remembrance,

LADY VISITANT
Prethee do not lose the pleasure of the World, for the sake of dull Contemplation.

LADY CONTEMPLATION
Why, the greatest pleasures that can be in Fruition, I take in Imagination: for whatsoever the sence enjoyes from outward objects, they may enjoy in inward thoughts. For the mind takes as much pleasure in creating of Fancies, as Nature to create and dissolve, and create Creatures anew: For Fancy is the Minds creature, & imaginations are as several worlds, wherein those Creatures are bred and born, live and dye; thus the mind is like infinite Nature.

LADY VISITANT
Prethee leave thy infinite folly.

LADY CONTEMPLATION
It is my infinite delight.

[Exeunt.

SCENE II

[Enter the Lady **POOR VIRTUE** weeping, and her **GOVERNESS**.

GOVERNESS
Madam, why do you weep, and grieve your self almost to death?

POOR VIRTUE

Have I not reason? my Father being kill'd, and I left friendlesse all alone, my Mother dying as soon as I was born.

GOVERNESS
There is no reason you should grieve for your Father, since he dyed in the defence of his King and Country.

POOR VIRTUE
Tis true, and I glory in his valiant loyal Actions, yet I cannot choose but mourn for the losse of his life, and weepe upon his death.

GOVERNESS
Methinks the greatest cause you have to weep, is, for the loss of your Estate, which the Enemy hath seized on, and you left only to live on Charity.

POOR VIRTUE
I cannot mourn for any thing that is in Fortunes power to take away.

GOVERNESS
Why? Fortune hath power on all things in the World.

POOR VIRTUE
O no, she hath power on nothing but base dross, and outward forms, things moveable; but she hath neither power on honest hearts, nor noble Souls; for 'tis the Gods infuse grace, and virtue; nor hath she power or Reason, or Understanding, for Nature creates, and disposes those; nor doth she govern Wisdome, for Wisdome governs her; nor hath she power on Life and Death, they are decreed by Heaven.

GOVERNESS
And will you weep at Heavens decree?

POOR VIRTUE
The Heavens decrees hinder not humanity, nor natural affection.

GOVERNESS
Well, ever since your Mother dyed, I have governed your Fathers House, and pleased him well; but since he is kill'd, and that there is nothing for me to govern, I will take my leave of you and seek another place; and I hope fortune will favour me so as to direct me to some Widdower, or old Batchelour, which desires a comely huswifly woman to order their private affairs.

POOR VIRTUE
I wish you all happiness, and if I were in a condition, I would make you a present.

[Exeunt.

SCENE III

[Enter **TWO GENTLEMEN**.

1ST GENTLEMAN
Sir, My Lord is so busy since his Fathers Death, with Stewards, Atturnies, and such like, about ordering his Estate, as I am loath to disturb him; but as soon as he hath done speaking to them, I will wait upon you to my Lord.

2ND GENTLEMAN
Sir, I shall wait my Lords leasure.

[Enter the **LADY WARD** and **NURSE CAREFUL**, they pass over the Stage.

2ND GENTLEMAN
Sir, what pretty young Lady is that which passes by?

1ST GENTLEMAN
She is a great Heiress, and was Ward to my old Lord, and he upon his Death-bed charged his Son my young Lord to marry her.

2ND GENTLEMAN
Surely small perswasions might serve turn; for her Beauty is
Rhetorick enough to perswade, nay to force affection.

1ST GENTLEMAN
Yet my Lord is discontented, he would rather choose for himself, than that his Father should have chosen for him; for it is the Nature of Mankind to reject that which is offered, though never so good; and to prize that they cannot get, although not worth the having.

2ND GENTLEMAN
Of what Quality, of Birth, and Nature, and disposition is she of?

1ST GENTLEMAN
She is Honourably Born, and seems to be of a sweet disposition; but of a Melancholy Nature.

[Enter a **SERVANT**.

SERVANT
Sir, my Lord desires the Gentleman would be pleased to walk in.

[Exeunt.

ACT II

SCENE I

[Enter the **LADY CONTEMPLATION**, and **SIR HUMPHREY INTERRUPTION**.

SIR HUMPHREY INTERRUPTION
Lady, what makes you so silently sad?

LADY CONTEMPLATION
Pardon me Sir, I am not sad at this time, for my thoughts are merry, and my spirits lively.

SIR HUMPHREY INTERRUPTION
There is no appearance of mirth in you, for mirth hath always a dancing heel, a singing voyce, a talking tongue, and a laughing face.

LADY CONTEMPLATION
I have such merry Companions sometimes; but I seldome dance, sing, talk, or laugh my self.

SIR HUMPHREY INTERRUPTION
Where are those Companions? I desire to be acquainted with them, and keep them Company.

LADY CONTEMPLATION
You cannot keep them Company, for the place they inhabit in, is too little for your corpulent body to enter; besides, they are so curious, choyce, and nice Creatures, as they will vanish at the very sight of you.

SIR HUMPHREY INTERRUPTION
Why Lady, I am none of the biggest sized Men, nor am I of a terrible aspect; I have seen very fine and delicate Creatures.

LADY CONTEMPLATION
But you never saw any of these Creatures.

SIR HUMPHREY INTERRUPTION
Pray where do they dwell, and what are their Names? I long to visit them.

LADY CONTEMPLATION
They dwell in my head, and their Sirnames are called thought, but how you will visit them I cannot tell, but they may visit you.

SIR HUMPHREY INTERRUPTION
Faith Lady, your relation hath made me despair of an enterview, but not a friendly entertainment, if you please to think well of me.

LADY CONTEMPLATION
Thoughts are free, and for the most part they censure according to fancy.

SIR HUMPHREY INTERRUPTION
Then fancy me such a one, as you could like best, and low most.

LADY CONTEMPLATION

That I cannot doe, for I love those best which I create my self, and Nature hath taught me to prize whatsoever is my own most, although of smaller valew, than what's anothers, although of greater worth.

SIR HUMPHREY INTERRUPTION

Then make me yours, by creating me anew.

LADY CONTEMPLATION

That is past my skill; but if you will leave me alone, I will think of you when you are gone; for I had rather of the two entertain you in my thoughts, than keep you Company in discourse, for I am better pleased with a solitary silence, or a silent solitariness, than with a talking conversation, or an entertaining talking, for words for the most part are rather useless spent, than profitably spoke, and time is lost in listning to them, for few tongues make Musick, wanting the Cords of Sense, or sound of Reason, or fingers of Fancy, to play thereon.

SIR HUMPHREY INTERRUPTION

But you will injure your wit, to bury your wit in solitary silence.

LADY CONTEMPLATION

Wit lives not on the tongue, as language doth, but in the brain, which power hath, as Nature, to create.

SIR HUMPHREY INTERRUPTION

But those are aery not material Creatures.

LADY CONTEMPLATION

'Tis true, but what they want in substance, they have in variety; for the brain can create Millions of several Worlds fill'd full of several Creatures, and though they last not long, yet are they quickly made, they need not length of time to give them form and shape.

SIR HUMPHREY INTERRUPTION

But there is required Speech to express them, or they are made in vain, if not divulged.

LADY CONTEMPLATION

Speech is an enemy to Fancy; for they that talk much, cannot have time to think much; and Fancies are produced from thoughts, as thoughts are from the minde, and the minde which doth create the thoughts, and the thoughts the fancies, is as a Deity; for it entertains it self with it self, and only takes pleasure in its own works, although none other should partake, or know thereof; but I shall talk a World out of my head, wherefore farewel.

[Exit.

SCENE II

[Enter **POOR VIRTUE**, and her Maid **NAN SCRAPEALL**.

NAN SCRAPEALL
Now your Estate is seized on, you have not means to keep a Servant, as to pay them for their service.

POOR VIRTUE
No truly Nan, but that which grieves me most, is, that I have not wherewithall to reward thee for thy past service.

NAN SCRAPEALL
I have served you these seven years, and have had nothing but my bare wages, unless it were some of the worst of your cast Clothes; for Mrs. Governess took order I should have none of the best; but I hope you will pay me my half years wages that is due to me.

POOR VIRTUE
Truly Nan I am not able, for not only my Estate, but all the Money, Jewels, Plate, and other goods you know was seized on, all that my Father left, or had a right to, unless it were my single self; and if you will take my service for half a year for payment, I will be very honest, dutiful, and diligent.

NAN SCRAPEALL
No by my troth, for you have been bred with so much attendance, curiosity, and plenty, as you will rather prove a charge than a payment; but if you can get means by your youth, and beauty, I shall come and claim what is owing me.

POOR VIRTUE
When I am able you shall not need to challenge it; for I will pay you before you ask.

[**NAN SCRAPEALL** goes out, and **POOR VIRTUE** sits down as in a deep study.

[Enter an old gray headed man namely **OLD HUMANITY**, who seeing her in so Melancholy a Posture, falls a weeping.

POOR VIRTUE
Why weepst thou old Humanity?

OLD HUMANITY
For the ruine of your noble family. I came a boy to your Grandmother the great and rich Lady Natures service, she being then newly married to your Grandfather the Lord Propriety; from whence sprung your Father the Lord Morality; your Grandfather, and Grandmother dying, I served your Father, who soon after married your Mother the Lady Piety, they living, whilst she lived, with Peace and Tranquillity; but she dying, left you only to your Father, as a pledg of their loves; and indeed, you are so like them both, as all must confess they were your Parents, although they knew not your Birth; and yet none can tell which you resembled most: thus have I lived to see your Grandfather, and Grandmother, and Father, and Mother dead, and Peace, and Tranquillity fled; and you sweet Virtue left dessolate and forlorn, both of friends and fortune; but sweet Lady comfort your self, for I have a little fortune, which I got honestly in your Fathers service; and as long as that lasts you shall not want.

POOR VIRTUE
I thank you, but you are old Humanity, and ready to go upon Crutches, and age and infirmities are shiftless; wherefore keep it for thy own use.

OLD HUMANITY

Why, so is unexperienced youth, both shiftless, and strengthless.

POOR VIRTUE

Tis true, yet youth hath an encreasing advantage; for time carryes youth up, but time pulls Age down; wherefore I will not take that from thee, that will cause thee to be the poorer, or hazard you to want; I shall only desire your advise, what I shall do, and what course I shall follow.

OLD HUMANITY

Alas sweet Lady, necessity will drive you into many extremities.

POOR VIRTUE

I shall have fortitude to arm me; but what Counsel will you give me?

OLD HUMANITY

The best way for you will be to get into some great Ladies service, and in such a place or office as to attend upon her Person, there you may live with honour and respect.

POOR VIRTUE

I had rather shrow'd my honest Poverty in a thatcht house, than live in a Palace to be pointed as for my misfortunes; for in this Age, misfortunes are accounted crimes, and poverty is condemned as a thief, and hang'd in the Chains of scorn; wherefore if I could get a service in an honest poor Farmers house, I might live happy, as being most obscure from the World, and the Worlds Vices; for vice encreases more in Palaces than in Cottages; for in Palaces Pride Plows, Faction Sowes, Riot Reaps, Extortion Threshes, Covetousness Whoords up the grain or gain; there youth is corrupted with Vanity, Beauty catcht with Flattery, Chastity endangered with Power, and Virtue slandered by Envy; besides, great Persons use their Servants too unequally, making them either Masters, or Slaves; where in an humble Cottage the industrious, and laborious Masters command their Servants friendly and kindly, and are obeyed with love; wherefore good Humanity, seek me out such a Place to live in, to serve.

OLD HUMANITY

I will, for I will never forsake you as long as I live, or at least so long as I have leggs to goe.

POOR VIRTUE

When you cannot visit me, I will visit you, for I shall never be ungrateful.

[Exit.

SCENE III

[Enter the **LADY CONVERSATION**, and **SIR EXPERIENCE TRAVELLER**.

LADY CONVERSATION

Sir Experience Traveller, you that have been so great a traveller, pray tell me what Nations have the rarest Beauties, and which the greatest Wits?

SIR EXPERIENCE TRAVELLER

In all my travels, the rarest Beauty that I have seen, and the greatest Wit that I have heard of, is your self, sweet Lady Conversation.

LADY CONVERSATION

Then you have lost your labour; for you might have seen my Beauty, and have heard my Wit, at lesse Charges, and more ease.

SIR EXPERIENCE TRAVELLER

Tis true Madam, had I only travelled to see a fair Lady, and hear a witty discourse.

LADY CONVERSATION

Why, many travel to lesse purpose.

SIR EXPERIENCE TRAVELLER

Tis true Madam, for some travel meerly to learn to make a leg or congy with a good grace, and to wear their cloaths, or acouster themselves fashionably. But I have observed in my travels, that very cold Countries, and very hot Countries, have neither so many Beauties, nor so much Wit, at lest not so much as more temperate Countries have.

LADY CONVERSATION

What is the reason of that?

SIR EXPERIENCE TRAVELLER

I cannot conceive the reason, unlesse the extream coldnesse of the Climate should congele their Spirits, and stupifie their Brains, making the Spirits unactive to get, and the Brain too barren to breed and bear Wit.

LADY CONVERSATION

So then you make the Spirits and the Brain the Parents to Wit.

SIR EXPERIENCE TRAVELLER

Yes Madam.

LADY CONVERSATION

And what reason give you for the scarcity of Beauties in very cold Climates?

SIR EXPERIENCE TRAVELLER

Beauty, Madam, is as tender and fading in the growth, as a Flower, although it be fresh and sweet; and the more delicate it is, the more subject to be nipt with the hard Frost, and to be withered with raw colds.

LADY CONVERSATION

Then hot Countries should produce good store.

SIR EXPERIENCE TRAVELLER

No Madam, for extream heat dryes up Wit, as water in a Spring, and Sun-burns beauty.

LADY CONVERSATION
But hot Brains are thought to produce the greatest Wits.

SIR EXPERIENCE TRAVELLER
Yes, if they be equally tempered with moisture; for as heat in moisture are Generators of all Creatures, so of Wit; but if the moisture exceed the heat, the Brain, or Mind becomes stupid, if the heat exceeds the moisture, the Brain or Mind becomes mad.

LADY CONVERSATION
What Nation hath the best Language?

SIR EXPERIENCE TRAVELLER
There are but three commendable things in Language, those are to be significant, copious, and smooth; and the English tongue hath the perfection of all, there being an oyle, or butter made of the cream of all other Languages. Thus, what with the Temperature of the Climate, and the soft, smooth, spreading, Language, England produces rarer Beauties, and eloquenter Orators, and finer Poets, than any other Nation in the world; and the Nobility and Gentry live not only in greater grandeur, than in other Nations, but naturally appear or look with a more splendid Greatnesse.

LADY CONVERSATION
Tis true, they did so in former times, when the Crown kept up Ceremony, and Ceremony the Crown; but since that Ceremony is down, their grandeur is lost, and their splendor put out; and no light thereof remains: But they are covered with a dark rudenesse, wherein the Clown justles the Lord, and the Lord gives the way to the Clown; the Man takes the wall of his Master, and the Master scrapes legs with Cap in hand to the Servant, and waits upon him, not out of a generous and noble Nature, but out of a base servile fear, and through fear hath given the Power away.

SIR EXPERIENCE TRAVELLER
I am sorry to hear the Nobility is so degenerated.

[Exit.

SCENE IV

[Enter the **LORD COURTSHIP**, and his Friend **MASTER ADVISER**.

MASTER ADVISER
I wonder your Lordship should be so troubled at your Fathers commands, which was to marry the Lady Ward, unlesse she had been ill-favoured and old.

LORD COURTSHIP
O that's the misery! that she is so young, For I had rather my Father had commanded me to marry one that had been very old, than one that is so young; for if she had been very old, there might have been some hopes of her death; but this young Filly will grow upon me, not from me; besides, those that are young give me no delight, their Company is dull.

MASTER ADVISER

Why, she is not so very young, she is fifteen years of Age.

LORD COURTSHIP

Give me a Lady to imbrace about the years of twenty, rather than fifteen; then is her Beauty like a full-blown Rose in June, her Wit like fruit is ripe and sweet, and pleasant to the ear; when those of fifteen are like to green sharp Fruit, not ripened by the Sun of Time. Yet that's not all that troubles me; but I cannot endure to be bound in Wedlocks shackles, for I love variety, and hate to be ty'd to one.

MASTER ADVISER

Why, you may have the more variety by marrying

LORD COURTSHIP

No faith, 'tis a Bar; for if I should but kisse my wives Maid which a thousand to one but I shall, my wife, if she doth not beat her Maid, making a hideous noise, with scoldings, yet she will pout, and cry, and feign her self sick, or else she would Cuckold me, and then I am paid for all.

MASTER ADVISER

Faith my Lord, it is a hundred to one but a man when he is marryed shall be Cuckolded, were he as wise as Solomon, as valiant as David, as fortunate as Ci¿½sar, as witty as Homer, or as handsome as Absalom; for Women are of the same Nature as men, for not one man amongst a thousand makes a good Husband, nor one woman amongst a thousand makes an honest Wife.

LORD COURTSHIP

No faith, you might well have put another Cypher and made it ten thousand.

MASTER ADVISER

Well my Lord, since you must marry, pray let me counsel you: This Lady Ward being very young, you may have her bred to your own Humour.

LORD COURTSHIP

How is that?

MASTER ADVISER

Why, accustome her to your wayes before you marry her; let her see your several Courtships to several Mistresses, and keep wenches in your house; and when she is bred up to the acquaintance of your customes, it will be as natural to her.

LORD COURTSHIP

What, to be a whore?

MASTER ADVISER

No, to know your humours, and to be contented thereat.

LORD COURTSHIP

Well, I will take your advice, although it is dangerous:
And as the old saying is, the Medicine may prove worse than the disease.

MASTER ADVISER
Why, the worst come to the worst, it is but parting.

LORD COURTSHIP
You say true; but yet a divorce will not clearly take off the disgrace of a Cuckold.

[Exit.

[Enter **POOR VIRTUE**, and **OLD HUMANITY**.

OLD HUMANITY
I have found out a service, a Farmer which hath the report of an honest labouring man, and his wife a good huswifely woman; they have onely one daughter about your years, a pretty Maid truely she is, and seems a modest one; but how you will endure such rough and rude work, which perchance they will imploy you in, I cannot tell, I doubt you will tire in it.

POOR VIRTUE
Do not fear, for what I want in strength, my industry shall supply.

OLD HUMANITY
But you must be fitted with cloaths according, and proper to your service.

POOR VIRTUE
That you must help me to.

OLD HUMANITY
That I will.

[Exit.

[Enter **SIR FANCY POET**, and the **LADY CONTEMPLATION**.

SIR FANCY POET
Sweet Lady Contemplation, although your thoughts be excellent, yet there are fine curiosities and sweet pleasures to be enjoyed in the use of the world.

LADY CONTEMPLATION

Perchance so, but would not you think that man a Fool that hath a great estate, a large convenient house, well situated, in sweet and healthfull Aire, pleasant and delightful, having all about for the eyes to view Landskips, and Prospects; beside, all the inside richly furnished, aud the Master plentifully served, and much company to passe his time with, as a resort of men of all Nations, of all Ages, of all qualities or degrees; and professions, of all humours, of all breedings, of all shapes, of all complexions: Likewise a recourse for all Wits, for all Scholars, for all Arts, for all Sciences; Also Lovers of all sorts Servants of all use, and imployments; Thus living luxuriously with all rarities and varieties, and yet shall go a begging, debasing himself with humble crouching, inslaving himself to Obligations, living upon cold Charity, and is denyed often times unkindly, or kickt out scornfully, when he may be honoured at home, and served in state, would not you think that this man had an inbred basenesse, that had rather serve unworthily, than command honourably; that had rather be inslaved, than free? Besides, that mind is a fool that cannot entertain it self with it's own thoughts; a wandring Vagabond, that is never, or seldome at home in Contemplation; A Prodigal to cast out his thoughts vainly in idle words, base to inslave it self to the Body, which is full of corruption, when it can create bodilesse Creatures like it self in Corporalities; with which self Creatures, it may nobly, honestly, freely, and delightfully entertain it self. With which, the mind may not only delight it self, but improve it self; for the thoughts; which are the actions of the mind, make the soul more healthful and strong by exercises; for the mind is the soules body, and the thoughts are the actions thereof.

SIR FANCY POET
After what manner will you form this Body?

LADY CONTEMPLATION
Thus, Understanding is the Brain, Reason the Liver, Love is the heart, Hate the Spleen, Knowledge the Stomach, Judgement the Sinews, Opinions the Bones, Will the Veins, Imaginations the Blood, Fancy the Spirits, the Thoughts are the Life, and Motion, or the Motions of the Life, the outward Form is the Mind it self, which sometimes is like a Beast, sometimes like a Man, and sometimes like a God.

SIR FANCY POET
And you my fair Goddesse.

[Exit.

SCENE II

[Enter the **LORD COURTSHIP**, and the **LADY AMOROUS**.

LADY AMOROUS
My Lord, you are too covetous to take a wife meerly for her riches.

LORD COURTSHIP
Believe me Madam, I do esteem of such Riches as Money, as I do of Marriage, and in my nature I do hate them both; for a man is enslaved by either: wherefore I would shun them if I could, and turn them out of doors, but that some sorts of necessity and conveniency inforce me to entertain them; the one for Posteritie sake, the other for subsistence of present life, besides convenient pleasures.

LADY AMOROUS
The Lady Ward, who is to be your wife, seems of a very dull disposition.

LORD COURTSHIP
She is so, but I like her the better for that, for I would have a deadly dull Wife, and a lively Mistresse, such a sprightly Lady as you are.

LADY AMOROUS
In truth my Lord, I am of a melancholy Nature.

LORD COURTSHIP
Certainly Madam, you onely know the Name, not the Nature, for your Nature is always fresh, and sweet, and pleasant, as the Spring.

LADY AMOROUS
O no, my mind is like to Winter, and my thoughts are numb and cold.

LORD COURTSHIP
If your thoughts were so cold, your words would be as if they were frozen between your lips, all your discourse would melt by drops, not flow so smoothly and swiftly into mens eares, as they at all times do.

LADY AMOROUS
Tis true, I am merry when I am in your company, but in your absence I am as dull as a cloudy day, and as melancholy as dark night.

LORD COURTSHIP
I cannot believe so well of my self, as that my company can be the light of your mirth, but I know that your company is the Sun of my life, nor could I live without it.

[Exit.

SCENE III

[Enter the **LORD TITLE**, **SIR EFFEMINATE LOVELY**, and **SIR GOLDEN RICHES**.

LORD TITLE
This is a barren Country, for in all this progresse I have not seen a pretty Country wench.

SIR EFFEMINATE LOVELY
Nor I.

SIR GOLDEN RICHES
Nor I.

LORD TITLE
If an person can tell, it is Tom Purveyer.

[Enter **TOM PURVEYOR**.

Now Tom Purveyer, are there no pretty wenches in this part of the Countrey?

TOM PURVEYOR
Yes that there are, an it please your Lorship, and not far off, two as pretty wenches as are in the Kingdome, and no dispraise to the rest.

[They all speak.

ALL
Where? where?

TOM PURVEYOR
Hard by here, at a Farmers House; the one is his Daughter, the other is his Servant-Maid.

ALL
Prethee Tom show us the house.

TOM PURVEYOR
Not all at once; but one after another.

ALL
Nay faith Tom, let us all see them at once; but we will Court them apart.

TOM PURVEYOR
Content.

[Exeunt.

SCENE IV

[Enter the **LADY CONVERSATION**, and **SIR FANCY POET**.

LADY CONVERSATION
What is the reason that Mercury is feign'd to be the patron of Thieves?

SIR FANCY POET
That is to be the patron of Scholars, for Scholars are the greatest Thieves, stealing from the Authours they read, to their own use.

LADY CONVERSATION
And why are Scholars counted the greatest Thieves?

SIR FANCY POET

Because that they steal the Spirits, or life of renown, out of the treasury of Fame; when all other sorts of Thieves steal but the goods of Fortune, which is nothing but a Corporal dross.

LADY CONVERSATION
And why is he feigned the talkative God?

SIR FANCY POET
Because Scholars talk more than other men, and most commonly so much, as they will let none speak but themselves; and when there is a Company of Scholars together, they will be so fierce in disputes, as they will be ready to go to cuffs for the Prerogative of their opinion.

LADY CONVERSATION
The Prerogative of the tongue you mean; but why are Scholars apt to talk most?

SIR FANCY POET
Because they overcharge their heads with several Authors, as Epicures do their Stomacks with variety of meats, and being overcharged, they are forced to vent it forth through the mouth, as the other through the gut; for the tongue, as a Feather, tickles the throat of Vainglory, vomiting out the slime of Learning, into the ears of the hearers; but some heads, as Stomacks which are naturally weak, are so grip'd, by reason it doth not digest well, as they vent nothing but windy Phrases; and other brains which are hot and moist, by reason of a facil memory, disgest so fast, as they do nothing but purge loose Sentences; and other brains that are too dry and Incipid, are so costive, as their restringency strains out nothing but strong lines.

LADY CONVERSATION
What is that, Non-sense?

SIR FANCY POET
Indeed they are hard words without sense.

LADY CONVERSATION
What makes a good Poet?

SIR FANCY POET
A quick Fancy.

LADY CONVERSATION
What makes a good Oratour?

SIR FANCY POET
A ready Tongue.

LADY CONVERSATION
What makes a good Physician?

SIR FANCY POET
Much Practice.

LADY CONVERSATION
What makes a good Divine?

SIR FANCY POET
A Holy Life.

LADY CONVERSATION
What makes a good States-Man?

SIR FANCY POET
Long experience, great observance, prudent industry, ingenuous wit, and distinguishing judgment.

LADY CONVERSATION
What makes a good Souldier?

SIR FANCY POET
Change of Fortune, Courage, Prudence, and Patience.

LADY CONVERSATION
What makes a good Courtier?

SIR FANCY POET
Diligence, Flattery, and time-serving.

LADY CONVERSATION
What makes a good Prince, or Governour?

SIR FANCY POET
Justice, Clemency, Generosity, Courage, and Prudence mixt together.

LADY CONVERSATION
What makes a good Woman?

SIR FANCY POET
A Poet.

LADY CONVERSATION
Why a Poet?

SIR FANCY POET
By reason the Poetical wits convert their natural defects into sweet graces, their follies to pure innocencies, and their Vices into Heroick Virtues.

LADY CONVERSATION
By these descriptions, you make as if women were more obliged to Poets than to Nature.

SIR FANCY POET

They are so; for where Nature, or Education, makes one good, or beautiful Woman, Poets make ten; besides, Poets have not only made greater numbers of beautiful women, but perfecter beauties than ever Nature made.

LADY CONVERSATION
Then let me tell you, that women make Poets; for women kindle the masculine brains with the fire of Love, from whence arises a Poetical flame; and their Beauty is the fuel that feeds it.

SIR FANCY POET
I confess, were there no women, there would be no Poets; for the Muses are of that Sex.

[Exeunt.

ACT IV

SCENE I

[Enter **ROGER FARMER**, and **MAUDLIN** his Wife.

MAUDLIN
Truly Husband our Maid Poor Virtue is a very industrious
Servant as ever I had in my life.

ROGER FARMER
Yes wife, but you were angry with me at first because I perswaded you to take her.

MAUDLIN
Why, she seem'd to be so fine a feat, as I thought she would never have setled to her work.

ROGER FARMER
Truly Wife, she does forecast her business so prudently, and doth every thing so orderly, and behaves her self so handsomely, and carryes her self so modestly, as she may be a Pattern to our Daughter.

MAUDLIN
I am a better Pattern my self.

[Exeunt.

SCENE II

[Enter **POOR VIRTUE** with a Sheephook, as coming from tending her sheep, and the **LORD TITLE** meets her.

LORD TITLE

Fair Maid, may I be your Shepheard to attend you.

POOR VIRTUE

I am but a single Sheep that needs no great attendance, and a harmless one, that strayes not forth the ground I am put to feed.

LORD TITLE

Mistake me not fair Maid, I desire to be your Shepheard, and you my fair Shepheardess, attending loving thoughts, that feed on kisses sweet, folded in amorous arms.

POOR VIRTUE

My mind never harbors wanton thoughts, nor sends immodest glances forth, nor will infold unlawful love, for chastity sticks as fast unto my Soul, as light unto the Sun, or heat unto the fire, or motion unto life, or absence unto death, or time unto eternity, and I glory more in being chast, than Hellen of her beauty, or Athens of their learning and eloquence, or the Lacedemonions of their Lawes, or the Persians of their Riches, or Greece of their Fables, or the Romans of their Conquests; and Chastity is more delightfull to my mind, than Fancy is to Poets, or Musick to the Ears, or Beauty to the Eyes, and I am as constant to Chastity, as truth to Unity, and Death to life; for I am as free, and pure from all unchastity as Angels are of sin

[**POOR VIRTUE** goes out.

[**LORD TITLE** alone.

LORD TITLE

I wonder not so much at Fortunes gifts, as Natures curiosities, not so much at Riches, Tittle and power, as Beauty, Wit, and Virtue, joyn'd in one; besides, she doth amaze me by expressing so much learning, as if she had been taught in some famous Schools, and had read many histories, and yet a Cottager, and a young Cottager, tis strange.

[Exit.

SCENE III

[Enter the **LORD COURTSHIP**, and **MASTER ADVISER**.

MASTER ADVISER
My Lord, doth my Counsel take good effect?

LORD COURTSHIP
Yes faith, for she seems to take it very patiently, or elce she is so dull a Creature as she is not sensible of any injury that's done her.

MASTER ADVISER
How doth she look when you adress, and salute your Mistriss?

LORD COURTSHIP
She seems to regard us not; but is as if she were in a deep contemplation of another world.

MASTER ADVISER
I think she is one of the fewest words, for I never heard her speak.

LORD COURTSHIP
Faith so few, as I am in good hope she is tongue-tyed, or will grow dumb.

MASTER ADVISER
That would be such a happiness, as all married men would envy you for.

LORD COURTSHIP
They will have cause, for there is nothing so tedious as talking women, they speak so constraintly, and utter their Nonsense with such formality, and ask impertinent questions so gravely, or else their discourse is snip snap, or so loud and shrill, as deafs a mans ears, so as a man would never keep them Company, if it were not for other reasons.

MASTER ADVISER
Your Lordship speaks as if you were a woman-hater.

LORD COURTSHIP
O Pardon me, for there is no man loves the Sex better than I; yet I had rather discourse with their beauty than their wits; besides, I only speak of generalities, not particularities.

[Exit.

SCENE IV

[Enter the **LADY CONTEMPLATION**, and **SIR HUMPHREY INTERRUPTION**.

SIR HUMPHREY INTERRUPTION
Lady, pray make me partaker of some of your conceptions.

LADY CONTEMPLATION
My conceptions are like the tongue of an extemporary Oratour, that after he hath spoke, if he were to speak upon the same subject he could hardly do it, if it were not impossible just to speak as he did, as to express the same subjects in the same expressions, and way of his natural Rhetorick; for the sense may be the same, but the expressions, & way of Rhetorick wil hardly be the same; but 'tis likely will be very different, and so differing, as not to be like the same; but the same premeditated Rhetorick, will many times serve to many several designs, or preaching, pleading, or speaking, the Theam or cause being altered; This is the difference betwixt extemporary Oratory, and premeditated Oratory, the one may be spoke, as many times as an Orator will, and, make the same Oratory serve to many several Subjects; the other being not fixt, but voluntary, vanishes out of the remembrance, the same many times do my conceptions.

SIR HUMPHREY INTERRUPTION

But I hope all are not vanished, some remain; wherefore pray expresse or present any one of your conceptions after what manner of way you please.

LADY CONTEMPLATION

Why then I will tell you, I had a conception of a Monster, as a Creature that had a rational soul, yet was a Fool: It had had a beautiful and perfect shape, yet was deformed and ill-favoured; It had clear distinguishing senses, and yet was sencelesse; It was produced from the Gods, but had the nature of a Devil; It had an eternal life, yet dyed as a Beast; It had a body, and no body.

SIR HUMPHREY INTERRUPTION

What Monster call you this?

LADY CONTEMPLATION

I call him Man.

SIR HUMPHREY INTERRUPTION

This is a Man of your own conception.

LADY CONTEMPLATION

A man of Natures creating is as monstrous for though man hath a rational soul, yet most men are fools, making no use of their reason; and though Man hath a beautiful and perfect shape, yet for the most part, they make themselves deformed and ill-favoured with antick postures, violent passions, or brutish vices; and man hath clear distinguishing Senses, yet in his sleep, or with fumes, or drink, he is sencelesse: Man was produced immediately from the Gods, yet man being wicked, and prone to evil, hath by evil wickednesse the nature of a Devil; Man 'tis said, shall live for ever, as having an eternal life, yet betwixt this life and the other, he dyes like a Beast, and turns to dust as other Creatures do; but the only difference between the man Nature creates, and the man my Conceptions create is, that Natures man hath a real substance as a real body; whereas my conceptive man is only an Idea, which is an incorporal man; so as the body of my concepted man, is as the soul of Natures created man, an incorporality.

[Exit.

SCENE V.

[Enter the **LORD TITLE**, and **MALL MEAN-BRED**.

1

LORD TITLE

Well, I have lost my first Course in Love, and now like an angry bloody Gray-hound, I will down with the first I meet, were she as innocent as a Dove, or as wise as a Serpent, down she goes.

[Enter **MALL MEAN-BRED**.

But soft, here's Loves game, and Ile flye at her. Fair One, for so you are.

MALL MEAN-BRED
Truly Sir I am but a Blouse.

LORD TITLE
Think better of your self, and believe me.

MALL MEAN-BRED
My Father hath told me, I must not believe a Gentleman in such matters.

LORD TITLE
Why sweetest? I am a Lord.

MALL MEAN-BRED
A Lord; Lord blesse your Worship then, but my Father gave me warning of a Lord, he said they might nay, say and swear too, and do any thing, for they were Peers of the Realm, there was no medling with them he said, without a Rebellion, blesse me from a Lord; for it is a naughty thing, as they say, I know not.

LORD TITLE
Do you value me so little, when I can make you an Apocryphal Lady?

MALL MEAN-BRED
The Apocrypha forsooth is out of my Book, I have been bred purer than to meddle with the Apocrypha, the Gods blesse us from it; and from all such ill things.

LORD TITLE
Well, in short, will you love me?

MALL MEAN-BRED
I am so ashamed to love a Lord forsooth that I know not how to behave my self.

LORD TITLE
I will teach you.

MALL MEAN-BRED
If your Honour will take the pains to teach a poor ignorant Country Maid, I will do the best I can to learn forsooth; but will it not be too much pains for your Honour, do you think?

LORD TITLE
No no, it will be both for my Honour; and my pleasure; and for the pleasure of my Honour.

MALL MEAN-BRED
Blesse us, how the Lords doe it backward and forward at their pleasure, the finest that ever was; but what would your Honour have of me?

LORD TITLE

By this kiss Ile tell you.

[He goes to kiss her, she seems nice and coy.

MALL MEAN-BRED
O fie, fie, good your Honour, do not standalize your lips to kisse mine, and make me so proud as never to kisse our Shepherd again.

[He offers.

MALL MEAN-BRED
No fie.

LORD TITLE
I will and must kisse you.

[He strives.

MALL MEAN-BRED
Nay, good your Honour, good your Honour.

[He kisses her.

What are you the better now? But I see there is no denying a Lord, forsooth it is not civil, and they are so peremptory too, the Gods blesse them, and make them their Servants.

LORD TITLE
This kisse hath so inflamed me, therefore for Loves sake, meet me in the Evening, in the Broom close here.

MALL MEAN-BRED
I know the Close forsooth, I have been there before now.

LORD TITLE
Well, and when we meet I will discover more than yet I have done.

MALL MEAN-BRED
So you had need forsooth, for nothing is discovered yet, either on your side, or mine, but I will keep my promise.

LORD TITLE
There spoke my better Angel; so adiew.

MALL MEAN-BRED
An Angel, I will not break my word for two angels, and I hope there will be no dew neither, God shield you forsooth.

[Exit.

2

[Enter **SIR EFFEMINATE LOVELY**, following **POOR VIRTUE**.

SIR EFFEMINATE LOVELY
Fair Maid, stay and look upon my person.

POOR VIRTUE
Why, so I do.

SIR EFFEMINATE LOVELY
And how do you like it?

POOR VIRTUE
As I like a curious built house, wherein lives a vain and self-conceited owner.

SIR EFFEMINATE LOVELY
And are not you in love with it?

POOR VIRTUE
No truly, no more than with a pencilled Picture.

SIR EFFEMINATE LOVELY
Why, I am not painted.

POOR VIRTUE
You are by Nature, though not by Art.

SIR EFFEMINATE LOVELY
And do you despise the best and curiousest Works of Nature?

POOR VIRTUE
No, I admire them.

SIR EFFEMINATE LOVELY
If you admire them, you will admire me, and if you admire me, you will yield to my desires.

POOR VIRTUE
There may be admiration without love, but to yield to your desires, were to abuse Natures Works.

SIR EFFEMINATE LOVELY
No, It were to enjoy them.

POOR VIRTUE

Nature hath made Reason in man, as well as Sence, and we ought not to abuse the one, to please the other; otherwise man would be like Beasts, following their sensualities, which Nature never made man to be; for she created Virtues in the Soul, to govern the Senses and Appetites of the Body, as Prudence, Justice, Temperance, and Conscience.

SIR EFFEMINATE LOVELY
Conscience? What is that, natural fear?

POOR VIRTUE
No, it is the tenderest part of the Soul, bathed in a holy dew, from whence repentant tears do flow.

SIR EFFEMINATE LOVELY
I find no such tender Constitution, nor moist Complexion in my Soul.

POOR VIRTUE
That is, by reason the Fire of unlawful Love hath drunk all up, & seared the Conscience dry.

SIR EFFEMINATE LOVELY
You may call it what Fire you will, but I am certain it is your Beauty that kindles it, and your Wit that makes it flame, burning with hot desires.

POOR VIRTUE
Pray Heaven my Virtue may quench it out again.

[**POOR VIRTUE** goes out.

[**SIR EFFEMINATE LOVELY** alone.

SIR EFFEMINATE LOVELY
I am sure Nature requires a self-satisfaction, as well as a self-preservation, and cannot, nor will not be quiet without it, esteeming it beyond life.

[Exit.

SCENE VII

[Enter the **LADY WARD**, and **NURSE CAREFUL**.

LADY WARD
I wonder my Lord Courtship, he being counted a wise man, should make me his Baud, if he intends to make me his Wife, and by my troth Nurse, I am too young for that grave Office.

NURSE CAREFUL
How ignorantly you speak Child? it is a sign you have been bred obscurely, and know little of the world; or rather it proves your Mother dyed before you could speak, or go, otherwise you would be better experienced in these businesses.

LADY WARD
My Mother, Nurse, Heaven rest her soul, she would never have made me a Baud.

NURSE CAREFUL
No, why then she would not do as most Mothers do now a dayes; for in this age Mothers bring up their daughters to carry Letters, and to receive messages, or at lest to watch at the door lest their Fathers should come unawares, and when they come to make some excuse, and then the Mother laughs, and sayes her daughter is a notable witty Girle.

LADY WARD
What, for telling a lye?

NURSE CAREFUL
Yes, when it is told so, as to appeare like a truth.

LADY WARD
But it is a double fault, as to deceive the Father, and be a Baud to the Mother.

NURSE CAREFUL
Why, the Mother will execute the same Office for the daughter when she is marryed, and her self grown into years; for from the age of seven or eight years old, to the time they are maryed, the Daughter is a Baud to the Mother; and from the time of their marriage, to the time of their Mothers death, the Mother is a Baud to the Daughter; but if the Mother be indifferently young, and hath a young tooth in her head, as the old saying is, they Baud for each other.

LADY WARD
But why doth not the Mother Baud for her Daughter, before she is marryed.

NURSE CAREFUL
O there is reason for that, for that may spoil her fortune, by hindering her marriage: for marriage is a Veile to cover the wanton face of adultery, the like Veil is Baud-mothers, and Baud-daughters; for who would suspect any lewdnesse, when the Mother and the Daughter is together?

LADY WARD
And are not Sons Pimps for their Fathers, as Daughters are for their Mothers?

NURSE CAREFUL
No faith, Boys have not facility, or ingenuity as Girles have; besides, they are kept most commonly so strictly to their Bookes, when Girles have nothing else to do; but when they have cast away their Books, and come to be marryed men, then they may chance to Pimp for their Wives.

LADY WARD
O fie Nurse, surely a man will never play the Pimp to Cuckold himself.

NURSE CAREFUL
O yes, if they be poor, or covetous, or ambitious; and then if they have a handsome woman to their wife, they will set her as a bait to catch their designs in the trap of Adultery; or patient, quiet, simple,

fearful men will, if they have a Spritely wife, they will play the Pimp, either for fear, or quiet; for such men to such wives, will do any thing to please them, although it be to Cuckold themselves.

LADY WARD
But surely Nurse no Gentleman will do so.

NURSE CAREFUL
I know not who you call Gentlemen, but those that bear up high and look big, and vant loud, and walk proud, and carry the out-side of a Gentleman, will do so.

LADY WARD
Certainly Nurse they are but Bastard Gentry; or else they are degenerated.

NURSE CAREFUL
An incipid Branch may spring from a sound Root, many a withered and rotten Plum may hang on a good Tree.

LADY WARD
And do Wives play the Bauds for their Husbands, as the Husbands play the Pimps for their Wives?

NURSE CAREFUL
Most often; for they will make Gossiping meetings, on purpose for their Husbands to Court other women; for they know when their Husbands minds are fill'd with amorous love, they will not muse upon their actions, nor examine their wayes; besides, when as the Husband would take his liberty without disturbance, he will wink at the liberty his wife takes, and so will be procurers for each other, and the Ladys acquaintance are Confidents.

LADY WARD
Confidents, what is that, Nurse?

NURSE CAREFUL
Why it is thus, two Ladies make friendship, or at least call Friends, and if any man desires to be a Courtly Servant to one of them, he addresses himself to the other, and expresses what Passions and Affections he hath for her friend, and so makes his complaints and affections known to her; whereupon she recommends his addresses and service to her Friend; thus doing a friendly Office by carrying and declaring his professions, and returning her Friends civil answers, appointing places for each others love-meetings, the other will do as much for her.

LADY WARD
Why this is a Baud.

NURSE CAREFUL
O peace Child, for if any body heard you say so, they would laugh at you for a Fool, but 'tis a sign you never was a Courtier, for I knew a young Lady that went to Court to be a Maid of Honour; and there were two young Ladies that were Confidents to each other, and a great Prince made love to one of them, but adddrest himself to the other, as being her Friend; this young Maid askt why he did so, it was answered, she was the Princes Mistresse Confident ; and just as you ask me, what said she, is a

confident a Baud; whereupon the whole Court laught at her, and for that only question condemned her to be a very Fool, nay, a meer Changling.

LADY WARD
Well Nurse, say what you will, Confident is but a Courtly name for a Baud.

[Exit.

SCENE VIII

[Enter **SIR EFFEMINATE LOVELY**, and **MALL MEAN-BRED**.

3

SIR EFFEMINATE LOVELY
Those wandering Stars that shine like brightest day, are fixt on me, the Center of your love.

MALL MEAN-BRED
O Heavens!

SIR EFFEMINATE LOVELY
Happy to touch those Lillies in your cheeks mingled with Roses, loves perfumed bath.

MALL MEAN-BRED
They grow forsooth in our Garden.

SIR EFFEMINATE LOVELY
You are the Garden of all sweets for love, your blushing lips of the Vermillion die, and those twin cherries, give me leave to taste.

MALL MEAN-BRED
Truly Sir, I understand no Latin, but I will call our Vicar to you, and he shall expound.

SIR EFFEMINATE LOVELY
No dearest Dear, my lovely Dear, my dearest Love, my lovelyest Dear.

MALL MEAN-BRED
I never cost you anything as yet, Sir.

SIR EFFEMINATE LOVELY
Why, then no Lady of Arcadie bred.

MALL MEAN-BRED
Truly Sir, this is as our Vicar saith, like Hebrew without poynts, to be read backwards; say any thing forward in Nottingham-shire; speak, that I may guess at, and I will answer your Worship, though truly, it is as fine as ever I understood not.

SIR EFFEMINATE LOVELY

Why then sweet heart I love you, and would gladly enjoy you.

MALL MEAN-BRED

O fie, enjoy is a naughty word forsooth, if it please you.

SIR EFFEMINATE LOVELY

It would please me, your thoughts of what you mince.

MALL MEAN-BRED

Thoughts are free forsooth, and I love whole joints without mincing.

SIR EFFEMINATE LOVELY

Why then in plain English, I would have your Maidenhead.

MALL MEAN-BRED

O dear, how will you get it, can you tell? Truely, truely, I did not think such naughty words would come forth of so fine a Gentlemans mouth.

SIR EFFEMINATE LOVELY

But tell me truely, do you think me fine?

MALL MEAN-BRED

You will make me blush now, and discover all; so fine cloaths, the Taylor of Norton never made such, and so finely made, unbuttoned and untrust doth so become you; but I do hang down my head for shame; and those Linnen Boot-hose (as if you did long to ride,) do so become you, and your short Coat to hang on your left arm; O sweet, O sweet; and then your Hat hid with so fine a Feather, our Peacocks tailes are not like it; and then your hair so long, so finely curled, and powder'd in sweets, a sweeter Gentleman I never saw. My love's beyond dissembling, so young, so fresh, so every thing, I warrant you; O Sir, you will ravish me, but yet you cannot.

SIR EFFEMINATE LOVELY

O how you have made me thankfulnesse all over for this your bounty to me; wherefore my earthly Paradise, let us meet in the next Close, there under some sweet Hedge to tast Loves aromatick Banquet at your Table.

MALL MEAN-BRED

O Sir, with blushes I consent; farewel; do not betray me then, you must not tell.
Farewell my sweetest, granting of my sute,
Shall still instave me, and be ever mute.

4

[Exit.

SCENE IX

[Enter **POOR VIRTUE**, and **SIR GOLDEN RICHES** following her.

SIR GOLDEN RICHES
Stay lovely Maid, and receive a Fortune.

POOR VIRTUE
I am Fortune proof Sir, she cannot tempt me.

SIR GOLDEN RICHES
But she may perswade you to reason.

POOR VIRTUE
That she seldome doth, for she is alwayes in extremes, and
Extremes are out of Reason's Schools,
That makes all those that follow Fortune Fooles.

SIR GOLDEN RICHES
What do you Rime, my pretty Maid?

POOR VIRTUE
Yes Rich Sir, to end my discourse.

SIR GOLDEN RICHES
I will make you Rich, if you will receive my gifts.

POOR VIRTUE
I love not gifts Sir, because they often prove bribes to corrupt.

SIR GOLDEN RICHES
Why, what do you love then?

POOR VIRTUE
I love Truth, Fidelity, Justice, Chastity; and I love obedience to lawful Authority, which rather than I
would willingly and knowingly infring, I would suffer death.

SIR GOLDEN RICHES
Are you so wilful?

POOR VIRTUE
No, I am so constant.

SIR GOLDEN RICHES
But young Maid, you ought not to deny all gifts, for there are gifts of pure affection, Love-gifts of
Charity, gifts of Humanity, and gifts of Generosity.

POOR VIRTUE

They are due debts, and not gifts; For those you call gifts of pure Love, are payments to dear deserving friends; and those of Charity are payments to Heaven; and those of Humanity are payments to Nature, and those of Generosity, are payments to Merit; but there are vain-glorious gifts, covetous gifts, gifts of fear, and gifts that serve as Bauds to corrupt foolish young Virgins.

SIR GOLDEN RICHES
Are you so wise to refuse them?

POOR VIRTUE
I am so virtuous as not to take them.

[Exit.

Notes
1 Written by my Lord Marquess of New-castle.
2 Here ends my Lord Marquesse.
3 This following Scene was writ by the Lord Marquess of New-castle.
4 Here ends my Lord Marquesse's Scene.

ACT V

SCENE I

[Enter the **LADY CONTEMPLATION**, and the **LADY VISITANT**.

LADY VISITANT
What still musing, O thou idle creature?

LADY CONTEMPLATION
I am not idle, for I busie my self with my own fancies.

LADY VISITANT
Fancies are like dust, soon raised, and suddenly blown away.

LADY CONTEMPLATION
No, they are as fire-works that sparkling flie about; or rather stars, set thick upon the brain, which gives a twinckling delight unto the mind.

LADY VISITANT
Prethee delight thy friends with thy conversation, and spend not thy time with dull thoughts.

LADY CONTEMPLATION
Pray give me leave to delight my self with my own thoughts, since I have no discourse to entertain a hearer.

LADY VISITANT

Why, your thoughts speak in your mind, although your tongue keeps silence.

LADY CONTEMPLATION
'Tis true; but they disturb not the mind with noise, for noise is the greatest enemy the mind hath: and as for my part, I think the most useless sense that Nature hath made, is hearing: the truth is, that hearing and smelling might well have been spared, for those two senses bring no materials into the brain; for sound and scent are incorporal.

LADY VISITANT
Then put out all the senses.

LADY CONTEMPLATION
There is no reason for that, for the eyes bring in pictures which serve the mind for patterns to draw new fancies by, and to cut, or carve out figurative thoughts, and the last serves towards the nourishment of the body, and touches the life.

LADY VISITANT
But wisedome comes through the ear by instruction.

LADY CONTEMPLATION
Wisedome comes through the eye by experience; for we shall doubt of what we only hear, but never doubt of what we see perfectly: But the ground of wisedom is Reason, and Reason is born with the soul, wherefore the ear serves only for reproof, and reproof displeases the mind, and seldome doth the life any good; nay many times it makes it worse, for the mind being displeased, grows angry, and being angry, malicious, and being malicious is revengeful, and revenge is war, and war is destruction.

LADY VISITANT
But if you were deaf, you would lose the sweet harmony of musick.

LADY CONTEMPLATION
Harmony becomes discord by often repetition, and at the best it doth but rock the thoughts asleep; whereas the mind takes more pleasure in the harmony of thoughts, and the musick of fancy, than in any that the senses can bring into it.

LADY VISITANT
Prethee let this harmonious musick cease for a time, and let us go and visit the Lady Conversation.

LADY CONTEMPLATION
It seems a strange humour to me, that all mankind in general should have an itching tongue to talk, and take more pleasure in the wagging thereof, than a beggar in scratching where a louse hath bit.

LADY VISITANT
Why, every part of the body was made for some use, and the tongue to express the sense of the mind.

LADY CONTEMPLATION
Pardon me, tongues were made for taste, not for words, for words wa an art which man invented: you may as well say, the hands were made to shuffle cards, or to do juggling tricks, when they were made to

defend and assist the body; or you may as well say, the leg were made to cut capers, when they were made to carry the body, and to move, as to goe from place to place; for, though the hands can shuffle cards, or juggle, and the legs can cut capers, yet they were not made by Nature for that use, nor to that purpose; but howsoever, for the most part, the sense and reason of the mind is lost in the number of words; for there are millions of words for a single figure of sense, and many times a cyphre of nonsense stands instead of a figure of sense: Besides, there are more spirits spent, and flesh wasted with speaking, than is got or kept with eating, as witness Preachers, Pleader, Players, and the like, who most commonly die with Consumptions; and I believe, many of our effeminate Sex do hurt the lungs with over-exercising of their tongues, not only with licking and tasting of Sweet-meats, but with chatting and prating, twitling and twatling; for I cannot say speaking, or discoursing, which are significant words, placed in a methodical order, then march in a regular body upon the ground of Reason, where sometimes the colour of Fancy is flying.

LADY VISITANT
Now the Flag of your wit is flying, is the fittest time to encounter the Lady Conversation ; and I make no question but you will be Victorious, and then you shall be Crowned the Queen of Wit.

LADY CONTEMPLATION
I had rather bury my self in a Monument of Thoughts, than sit in the Throne of Applause for Talking.

[Exeunt.

SCENE II

[Enter the **LORD TITLE** to **POOR VIRTUE,** who sat under a little hedge, bending like a Bower. He sits down by her.

LORD TITLE
Sweet, why sit you so silently here?

POOR VIRTUE
My speech is buried in my thoughts.

LORD TITLE
This silent place begets melancholy thoughts.

POOR VIRTUE
And I love melancholy so well, as I would have all as silent without me, as my thoughts are within me; and I am so well pleased with thoughts, as noise begets a grief, when it disturbs them.

LORD TITLE
But most commonly Shepherds and Shepherdesses sit and sing to pass away the time.

POOR VIRTUE
Misfortunes have untuned my voice, and broke the strings of mirth.

LORD TITLE

Misfortunes? what misfortunes art thou capable of? Thou hast all thou wert born to.

POOR VIRTUE

I was born to die, and 'tis misfortune enough I live, since my life can do no good: I am but useless here.

LORD TITLE

You were born to help increase the world.

POOR VIRTUE

The world needs no increase, there are too many creatures already, especially mankinde; for there are more than can live quietly in the world; for I perceive, the more populous, the more vicious.

LORD TITLE

'Tis strange you should be so young, so fair, so witty as you are, and yet so melancholy; thy poverty cannot make it, for thou never knewest the pleasure of riches.

POOR VIRTUE

Melancholy is the only hopes I do rely upon, that though I am poor, yet that may make me wise; for fools are most commonly merriest, because they understand not the follies that dwell therein, nor have enough considerations of the unhappiness of man, who hath endless desires, unprofitable travels; hard labours, restless hours, short pleasures, tedious pains, little delights, blasted joys, uncertain lives, and decreed deaths; and what is mirth good for? it cannot save a dying friend, nor help a ruined Kingdome, nor bring in plexy to a famished Land; nor quench out malignant Plagues; nor is it a ward to keep misfortunes off, though it may triumph on them.

LORD TITLE

But you a young Maid, should do as young Maids do, seek out the company of young Men.

POOR VIRTUE

Young Maids may save themselves that labour, for Men will seek out them, or else you would not be sitting here with me.

LORD TITLE

And are you not pleas'd with my company?

POOR VIRTUE

What pleasure can there be in fears?

LORD TITLE

Are you afraid of me?

POOR VIRTUE

Yes truly; for the ill example of men, corrupts the good principles in women: But I fear not perverting of my Vertue, but mens incivilities.

LORD TITLE

They must be very rudely bred, that give you not respect, you being so very modest.

POOR VIRTUE

'Tis not enough to be chastly modest and honest, but as a servant to my Mr. and Mrs. I must be dutiful, and careful to their commands, and on their employments they have put to me: wherefore I must leave you Sir, and go fold my sheep.

LORD TITLE

I will help you.

[Exeunt.

[Enter **SIR GOLDEN RICHES**, and **MALL MEAN-BRED**.

1

SIR GOLDEN RICHES

Sweet-heart, I have no Sonnets, Songs, or stronger Lines, with softer Poesie to melt your Soul, nor Rhetorick to charm your Eares, or Logick for to force, or ravish you, nor lap't in richer cloaths embalm'd in Sweets, nor Courtly Language; but am an Ancient Squire, by name Sir Golden Riches, which hath force in all things, and then in Love; for Cupid being blinde, he is for feeling, and look here my Wench, this purse is stuff'd with Gold, a hundred pounds.

MALL MEAN-BRED

Let me see, poure it on the ground.

SIR GOLDEN RICHES

I will obey thee: Look here my Girl.

[He poures it on the ground.

MALL MEAN-BRED

O dear, how it doth shine forsooth! it almost blinds mine eyes; take it away, yet pray let it stay: truly I know not what to do with it.

SIR GOLDEN RICHES

No? why it will buy you rich Gowns, lapp'd in the Silk-worms toyls, with stockings of the softer silk, to draw on your finer legs, with rich lace shooes, with roses that seem sweet, and garters laced with spangles like twinckling Stars, embalm your hair with Gessimond Pomatums, and rain Odoriferous Powders of proud Rome.

MALL MEAN-BRED

O Heaven! what a Wench shall I be, could I get them! But shall we have fine things of the Pedlar too?

SIR GOLDEN RICHES

Buy all their packs, and send them empty home.

MALL MEAN-BRED
O mighty! I shall put down all the Wenches at the May-pole; then what will the Bag-piper say, do you think? Pray tell me, for he is a jeering knave.

SIR GOLDEN RICHES
Despise the Rural company, and that windy bag, change it for Balls with greatest. Lords to dance, and bring the Jerkin Fiddles out of frame.

MALL MEAN-BRED
Then I shall have a Mail-Pillion, and ride behind our Thomas to the dancing.

SIR GOLDEN RICHES
No, you shall ride in rich gilt Coaches, Pages and Lacquies in rich Liveries, with Gentlemen well cloath'd, to wait upon you.

MALL MEAN-BRED
And be a Lady; then I will be proud, and will not know Thomas any more, nor any Maid that was acquainted with me.

SIR GOLDEN RICHES
You must forget all those of your Fathers house too; for I'll get a Pedigree shall fit you, and bring you Lineally descended from Great Charlemain.

MALL MEAN-BRED
No, I will have it from Charls wayn my Fathers Carter; but I would so fain be a Lady, and it might be: I will be stately, laugh without a cause, and then I am witty, and jeer sometimes, and speak nonsense aloud. But this Gold will not serve for all these fine things.

SIR GOLDEN RICHES
Why then we will have hundreds and thousands of pounds, until you be pleas'd, so I may but enjoy you in my Arms.

MALL MEAN-BRED
No Maid alive can hold out these Assaults, Gold is the Petarr that breaks the Virgins gates, a Souldier told me so. Well then, my Lord Title, farewel, for you are an empty name; and Sir Effeminate Lovely, go you to your Taylor, make more fine cloaths in vain.
I'll stick to Riches, do then what you will,
The neerest way to pleasure buy it still.

[Exeunt.

SCENE IV

[Enter the **LADY WARD** alone.

LADY WARD

Why should Lord Courtship dislike me? Time hath not plowed wrinkles in my face, not digged hollows in my cheeks, not hath he set mine eyes deep in my head, nor shrunk my sinews up, nor suck'd my veins dry, nor fed upon my flesh, making my body insipid and bate; neither hath he quenched out my wit, nor decay'd my memory, nor ruin'd my understanding; but perchance Lord Courtship likes nothing but what is in perfection; and I am like a house which Time hath not fully finished, nor Education throughly furnished.

SCENE V

[Enter **POOR VIRTUE**, and **SIR GOLDEN RICHES** meets her coming from **MALL MEAN-BRED**.

SIR GOLDEN RICHES

Sweet-heart, refuse not Riches, it will buy thee friends, pacifie thy enemies; it will guard thee from those dangers that throng upon the life of every creature.

POOR VIRTUE

Heavenly Providence is the Marshal which makes way for the life to pass through the croud of dangers, and my Vertue will gain me honest friends, which will never forsake me, and my humble submission will pacifie my enemies, were they never so cruel.

SIR GOLDEN RICHES

But Riches will give thee delight, and place thee in the midst of pleasures.

POOR VIRTUE

No, it is a peaceable habitation, a quiet and sound sleep, and a healthful body, that gives delight and pleasure, and 'tis not riches; but riches many times destroy the life of the body, or the reason in the soul, or, at least, bring infirmities thereto through luxury; for luxury slackens the Nerves, quenches the Spirits, and drowns the Brain, and slackned Nerves make weak Bodies, quenched Spirits, timotous Minds, a drowned Brain, a warry Understanding, which causeth Sloth, Effeminacy, and Simplicity.

SIR GOLDEN RICHES

How come you to know so much of the world, and yet know so few passages in it, living obscurely in a Farmers house?

POOR VIRTUE

The Astronomers can measure the distance of the Planets, and take the compass of the Globe, yet never travel to them, not have they Embassadors from them, nor Liegers to lie therein to give Intelligence.

SIR GOLDEN RICHES

How come you to be so learnedly judicious, being so young, poor, and meanly born and bred?

POOR VIRTUE

Why, Fire, Air, Water, and Earth, Animals, Vegetables, and Minerals, are Volumes large enough to express Nature, and make a Scholar learn to know the course of her works, and to understand many effects produced therefrom. And as for Judgment and Wit, they are brother and sister; and although they do not alwayes, and at all times agree, yet are they alwayes the children of the Brain, being begot by Nature. Thus what Wit or Knowledge I have, may come immediately from Nature, not from my Birth or Breeding, but howsoever, I am not what I seem.

[Exeunt.

SCENE VI

[Enter the **LADY CONTEMPLATION**, and the **LADY VISITANT**.

LADY VISITANT
What makes you look so sad?

LADY CONTEMPLATION
Why Monsieur Amorous 's visit hath been the cause of the death of one of the finest Gentlemen of this Age.

LADY VISITANT
How, pray?

LADY CONTEMPLATION
Why thus; my Imagination (for Imagination can Create both Masculine and Feminine Lovers) had Created a Gentleman that was handsomer and more beautiful than Leander, Adonis, or Narcissus ; valianter than Tamberlain, Scanderbeg, Hannibal, Cï¿½sar, or Alexander ; sweeter-natur'd than Titus, the delight of mankinde; better-spoken, and more eloquent than Tully, or Demosthenes ; wittyer than Ovid, and a better Poet than Homer. This man to fall desperately in love with me, as loving my Vertues, honouring my Merits, admiring my Beauty, wondring at my Wit, doting on my Person, adoring me as an Angel, worshipping me as a Goddess; I was his Life, his Soul, his Heaven. This Lover courted my affection; with all the industry of Life, gifts of Fortune, and actions of Honour; sued for my favour, as if he had sued to Heaven for mercy; but I, as many cruel goddesses do, would neither receive his obligations, nor regard his vowes, nor pity his tears, not hearken to his complaints, but rejected his Sute, and gave him an absolute denyal; whereupon he was resolved to dye, as believing no torments could be compared to those of my disdain; and since I would not love him living, he hoped by dying, his death might move my pity, and so beget a compassionate remembrance from me; where upon he got secretly neer my chamber-door, and hung himself just where I must go out, which when I saw, I started back in a great fright, but at last running forth to call for help to cut him down, in came Monsieur Amorous, which hinderance made me leave him hanging there, as being ashamed to own my cruelty; and he hath been talking, or rather prating here so long, as by this time my kind Love is dead.

LADY VISITANT
O no, for Lovers will hang a long time before they dye; for their necks are tuff, and their hearts are large and hot.

LADY CONTEMPLATION
Well, pray leave me alone, that I may cut him down, and give him Cordials to restore life.

LADY VISITANT

Faith you must let him hang a little time longer, for I have undertaken to make you a sociable Lady this day; wherefore you must goe abroad to a friends house with me.

LADY CONTEMPLATION

Who I? what do you think I will goe abroad, and leave my Lover in a twisted string? his legs hanging dangling down, his face all black and swelled, and his eyes almost started out of his head? no, no, pray goe alone by your self, and leave me to my Contemplation.

LADY VISITANT

Well, if you will not goe, I will never see you, nor be friends with you again.

LADY CONTEMPLATION

Pray be not angry, for I will go, if you will have me, although I shall be but a dull companion; for I shall not speak one word; for wheresoever I am, my thoughts will use all their Industry to cut the string, and take him down, and rub and chase him against a hot fire.

LADY VISITANT

Come, come, you shall heat your self with dancing, and let your Lover hang.

LADY CONTEMPLATION

That I cannot; for active bodies and active brains are never at once, the one disturbs the other.

LADY VISITANT

Then it seems you had rather have an active brain, than an active body.

LADY CONTEMPLATION

Yes; for when the brain doth work, the understanding is inriched, and knowledge is gained thereby: whereas the body doth oft-times waste the life with too much exercise.

LADY VISITANT

Take heed you do not distemper your brain with too much exercising your thoughts.

LADY CONTEMPLATION

All distempers proceed from the body, and not from the minde; for the minde would be well, did not the humours and appetites of the body force it into a distemper.

LADY VISITANT

Well, upon the condition you will goe, you shall sit still, and your wit shall be the Musick.

LADY CONTEMPLATION

Prethee let me rest at home; for to day the strings of my wit are broken, and my tongue, like a fiddle, is out of tune: Besides, Contemplative persons are at all times dull speakers, although they are pleasant thinkers.

[Exeunt.

Notes
1 This Scene was written by my Lord Marquiss of Newcastle.

Margaret Cavendish – A Concise Bibliography

Philosophical Fancies (1653)
Poems and Fancies (1653)
Philosophical and Physical Opinions (1655)
Nature's Pictures drawn by Fancie's Pencil to the Life (1656)
The World's Olio (1655)
Playes, (1662) folio, containing twenty-one plays including
Loves Adventures
The Several Wits
Youths Glory, and Deaths Banquet
The Lady Contemplation
Wits Cabal
The Unnatural Tragedy
The Public Wooing
The Matrimonial Trouble
Nature's Three Daughters, Beauty, Love and Wit
The Religious
The Comical Hash
Bell in Campo
A Comedy of the Apocryphal Ladies
The Female Academy
Plays never before printed (1668), containing five plays.
The Sociable Companions, or the Female Wits
The Presence
The Bridals
The Convent of Pleasure
A Piece of a Play
Orations of Divers Sorts (1662)
Philosophical Letters, or Modest Reflections upon some Opinions in Natural Philosophy maintained by several learned authors of the age (1664)
CCXI Sociable Letters (1664)
Observations upon Experimental Philosophy & Description of a New World (1666)
The Blazing World (1666)
The Life of William Cavendish, Duke, Marquis, and Earl of Newcastle, Earl of Ogle, Viscount Mansfield, and Baron of Bolsover, of Ogle, Bothal, and Hepple, &c. (1667)
Grounds of Natural Philosophy (1668)

www.ingramcontent.com/pod-product-compliance
Lightning Source LLC
Chambersburg PA
CBHW021945040426

42448CB00008B/1245